work songs

Exploring frustration, compromise, stress and joy from the Psalms

by Tim Chester

thegoodbook
COMPANY

work songs
a good book guide on the psalms
© Tim Chester/The Good Book Company, 2006. Reprinted 2011
Series Consultants: Tim Chester, Carl Laferton, Tim Thornborough, Anne Woodcock

The Good Book Company
Tel (UK): 0345-225-0880
Tel (int): + (44) 208-942-0880
Tel: (US): 866 244 2165
Email: admin@thegoodbook.co.uk

Websites
UK: www.thegoodbook.co.uk
N America: www.thegoodbook.com
Australia: www.thegoodbook.com.au
New Zealand: www.thegoodbook.co.nz

ISBN: 9781905564675

Printed in China

CONTENTS

introduction: good book guides

Every Bible-study group is different—yours may take place in a church building, in a home or in a cafe, on a train, over a leisurely mid-morning coffee or squashed into a 30-minute lunch break. Your group may include new Christians, mature Christians, non-Christians, mums and tots, students, businessmen or teens. That's why we've designed these *Good Book Guides* to be flexible for use in many different situations.

Our aim in each session is to uncover the meaning of a passage, and see how it fits into the "big picture" of the Bible. But that can never be the end. We also need to appropriately apply what we have discovered to our lives. Let's take a look at what is included:

⊕ **Talkabout:** Most groups need to "break the ice" at the beginning of a session, and here's the question that will do that. It's designed to get people talking around a subject that will be covered in the course of the Bible study.

⊕ **Investigate:** The Bible text for each session is broken up into manageable chunks, with questions that aim to help you understand what the passage is about. **The Leader's Guide** contains **guidance on questions**, and sometimes ⊗ additional "follow-up" questions.

⊕ **Explore more (optional):** These questions will help you connect what you have learned to other parts of the Bible, so you can begin to fit it all together like a jig-saw; or occasionally look at a part of the passage that's not dealt with in detail in the main study.

⊕ **Apply:** As you go through a Bible study, you'll keep coming across **apply** sections. These are questions to get the group discussing what the Bible teaching means in practice for you and your church. ⊡ **Getting personal** is an opportunity for you to think, plan and pray about the changes that you personally may need to make as a result of what you have learned.

⊕ **Pray:** We want to encourage prayer that is rooted in God's word—in line with His concerns, purposes and promises. So each session ends with an opportunity to review the truths and challenges highlighted by the Bible study, and turn them into prayers of request and thanksgiving.

The **Leader's Guide** and introduction provide historical background information, explanations of the Bible texts for each session, ideas for **optional extra** activities, and guidance on how best to help people uncover the truths of God's word.

why study Work Songs?

In the Disney version of Snow White, the seven dwarfs go off to work each morning singing happily. These studies look at six psalms to sing in the workplace. For many Christians there is a gap between church on Sunday and work on Monday. These psalms will help you bridge that gap. They re-tune our hearts to the new song of God's redemption (see Psalm 40 v 3).

There is an annual "take your daughter to work" day. The aim is for girls to experience the world of work and break down prejudices about women's roles. These psalms will help us take our God to work—or maybe discover that He is already present in the workplace.

They address the frustration we often feel with work, the temptations to compromise, the busyness and stress of the workplace, and the sometimes overwhelming expectations of colleagues. They also give something to sing on fantastic days when everything goes brilliantly!

Use these studies to encourage yourself, or, if you have some Christian colleagues, why not gather them together, to bring the richness, truth and insight of God's word to bear on your daily grind?

These Bible studies offer more of a thematic journey through selected psalms, rather than an attempt to offer a complete understanding of each of these Spirit-inspired songs. The studies focus on aspects of the psalms that relate to issues we face in our everyday working lives.

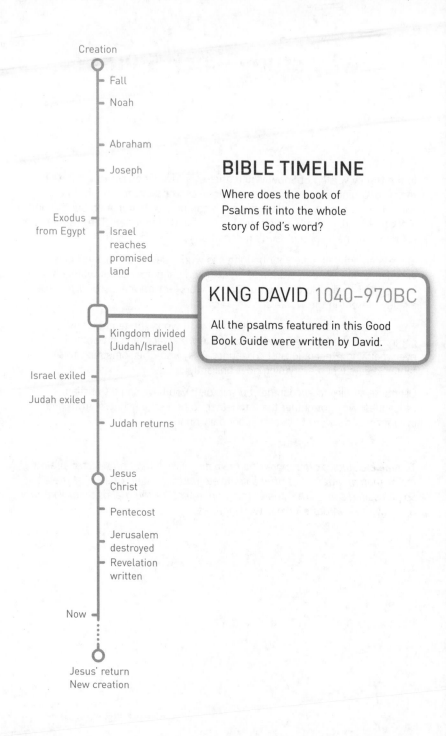

Creation

Fall

Noah

Abraham

Joseph

Exodus from Egypt

Israel reaches promised land

BIBLE TIMELINE

Where does the book of Psalms fit into the whole story of God's word?

KING DAVID 1040–970BC

All the psalms featured in this Good Book Guide were written by David.

Kingdom divided (Judah/Israel)

Israel exiled

Judah exiled

Judah returns

Jesus Christ

Pentecost

Jerusalem destroyed

Revelation written

Now

Jesus' return
New creation

1

Psalm 8

A SONG FOR YOUR JOURNEY TO WORK

⊕ talkabout

1. How do you usually feel on your journey to work in the morning?

2. Why do you work?

⊕ investigate

> **Read Psalm 8**

3. Look at v 1-3. God is a worker (v 3). How do we see the majesty of God's name in what He has made?

4. How should we respond to God's work (v 2)?

5. God is a worker! How can that truth change our attitude to work?

⊡ **explore more**

› **Read Matthew 21 v 1-17**

optional

How does Jesus use Psalm 8 v 2 to rebuke the religious leaders?
Why does He do so?
What does the rest of Psalm 8 v 2 add to our understanding of what is happening in Matthew 21?

6. Look at verses 3-4. What is the point of the comparison between God and humanity that the writer makes?

⊡ **getting personal**

Do you ever feel small in the universe?
Do you ever feel your work is insignificant?
Think of a time when your "smallness" has been very apparent to you.

7. Look at verses 5-9. What is the position God has given to us in His world?

⊡ **explore more**

> **Read Psalm 104 v 1-24**

What are the signs that God has created an ordered world?

What is humanity's place in that order? What is our role?

optional

⊟ apply

God gives humanity the job of ruling His world under His rule (Genesis 1 v 26-28). We are to care for it as stewards of God's good creation.

8. What significance does this give to our work?

9. How would you rate humanity's performance as stewards of God's world?

Humanity has rejected God, so we do not rule God's world under God. As a result, work is often frustrating, oppressive and futile.

⊡ investigate

> **Read Hebrews 2 v 5-9**

10. Look at verse 8. What is the writer's verdict on humanity's stewardship?

DICTIONARY

Subjected (v 2): given to rule.
Grace (v 9): undeserved kindness.

11. What is God's solution (v 9)? **See also 1 Corinthians 15 v 20-28.**

⊟ **apply**

12. How will our hope in Jesus transform the way we think about our work? **See Romans 8 v 19-22.**

13. How should following Jesus transform our work in the present? **See also Colossians 3 v 22-25 and Titus 2 v 9-10.**

⊕ **pray**

Use Psalm 111 to praise God the worker for the work He has done.

Pray that, even when work is frustrating, oppressive or futile, you may have a sense of working for God and His glory.

2 Psalm 5
A SONG FOR MISERABLE MONDAYS

⊕ talkabout

1. What problems do you face as a Christian in the workplace?

Often it feels as if there is a huge gap between Sunday mornings and Monday mornings. On Sunday we sing of God's goodness and power; on Monday we dance to a different tune. God seems close to us on Sunday morning, but seems far away from the gossip, backbiting and scheming of Monday. Sometimes we find ourselves the victim of godless talk; sometimes we get caught up in it. Psalm 5 is for these Monday mornings.

⊡ getting personal

Is there a gap between your behaviour and attitude on Sunday morning and Monday morning? Would the people who see you on Sunday morning notice a difference if they saw you on Monday morning? Would the people who see you on Monday morning notice a difference if they saw you on Sunday morning?

⬇ investigate

❯ Read Psalm 5

2. How do verses 1-3 help us bridge the gap between Sunday and Monday mornings?

DICTIONARY

Abhors (v 6): really hates.
Temple (v 7): where God is particularly present.
Righteousness (v 8): in this context, living the right way, God's way.
Righteous (v 12): those who are right with God through trusting in His promises and seeking to live His way.

3. Imagine verses 4-6 were displayed on the wall of your workplace. What difference would they make? What difference would they make to you?

4. Look at verse 7 and **John 2 v 19-22**. What does it mean for us today to bow towards the temple?

5. Look at verses 7-8. What is the solution to living among wicked people?

6. Look at verses 6 and 9-10. What lies are told at your workplace?

⊖ **apply**

7. Look at verses 11-12. How can we be distinctive in a world often filled with deceit, intrigues and gossip?

8. Look at verse 3. How often do we need to renew a God-centred perspective on our workplace? How can we do this?

⊕ **investigate**

Psalm 5 talks about "the wicked" (v 4) and "the righteous" (v 12).

▶ **Read Romans 3 v 9-20**

9. Romans 3 quotes Psalm 5 and other Bible references—to show what?

> **DICTIONARY**
>
> **Gentiles (v 9):** non-Jews.
> **Fear (v 18):** right respect and awe for someone.
> **Law (v 19-20):** the way God commands people to live in His world.

▶ Read Romans 3 v 21-26

10. How can we be righteous, according to this passage?

⤳ apply

We do not need to prove or justify ourselves because God makes us righteous through the death of Jesus. People at work may not be trying to make themselves right with God. But they are often trying to prove themselves or gain a secular version of salvation (fulfilment, identity, meaning, approval).

11. How do you see this in your colleagues?

12. How do you see this in yourself?

13. What difference can the good news of justification by faith make in your workplace?

↥ pray

Use verses 11-12 to pray about the problems and temptations that you face in the workplace:

Let all who take refuge in you be glad;
let them ever sing for joy.
Spread your protection over them,
that those who love your name may rejoice in you.
For surely, O LORD, you bless the righteous;
you surround them with your favour as with a shield.

3 Psalm 37
A SONG FOR TEMPTING TUESDAYS

⊕ talkabout

1. What temptations do you face at work?

We are often tempted to compromise our Christian values in the workplace: to scheme a little; to take advantage of others; to be economical with the truth. It doesn't help that we see other people who do these things getting on as a result. Even if we don't compromise, we often get angry that others get away with it, or fret about the consequences to us. David talks about these kinds of temptations in Psalm 37.

⊙ investigate

❯ Read Psalm 37

2. What do the wicked do (try to find at least six things)?

3. What happens to the wicked in the short term?

4. How have you seen people getting on in life by doing wrong?

5. What happens to the wicked in the long term?

6. When will this happen?

7. What does David say the LORD will do for the righteous?

We live in a moral universe, in which actions have consequences. It doesn't always seem like that. But sooner or later God punishes evil and rewards goodness.

8. Look at verses 1-7. How are we to relate to the LORD?

→ **apply**

9. What does this mean for you in your work situation?

10. Look at verses 8-9. How do you feel when you see other people getting on in life by doing wrong?

11. How can trusting and delighting in God help you cope better with these feelings?

⊍ investigate

12. What is the desire of the person described in verse 4? What is God's promise to them?

13. Look for references in the psalm to the promised land.

14. Jesus quotes from this psalm in **Matthew 5 v 5**. What does He do to the promise of blessing in the land?

15. What is the future for those who trust in the LORD?

➔ apply

This psalm is an acrostic poem. Each section begins with the successive letters of the Hebrew alphabet. This would have made it easier to remember.

16. What are you going to remember from this psalm?

17. How are you going to remember it in your workplace next time you are tempted to compromise?

🙂 getting personal

Verse 31 says: "The law of his God is in his heart; his feet do not slip". The truths of this psalm will stop us slipping into sin when we face temptation. What can you do to ensure God's word is in your heart?

⬆ pray

- Trust in the LORD (v 3).
- Delight in the LORD (v 4).
- Commit your way to the LORD (v 5).
- Be still before the LORD (v 7).
- Hope in the LORD (v 9).

Use each of these expressions to pray for one another in the workplace.

Close with the confident words of verses 39-40:

The salvation of the righteous comes from the LORD;
he is their stronghold in time of trouble.
The LORD helps them and delivers them;
he delivers them from the wicked and saves them,
because they take refuge in him.

4 Psalm 62
A SONG FOR WORKAHOLIC WEDNESDAYS

⊕ talkabout

1. Why is life today so busy?

2. Is it bad to be busy?

⊕ investigate

❯ Read Psalm 62

Look at verses 1-4. We are often too busy because we are worried about the future, or we want to be in control of our lives.

DICTIONARY

Extortion (v 10): getting something (usually money) through threats or force.

3. Where have you seen these pressures to be busy in yourself or other people?

4. What particular problems did David face?

5. How would you expect someone to react in this situation?

6. But how does David react in this situation?

7. Why does David react in this way?

⊡ explore more

> **❯ Read Psalm 127**

Look at verses 1-2.
Do you often get up early to get ahead? Or often stay up late to finish? What's Solomon's verdict on worry-induced overwork? What's his remedy?

Look at verses 3-5.
Do you worry about your family's future? What behaviour does this worry produce? What do you think Solomon would say to you?

Look at verses 5-9. We are often too busy because we are worried about our reputation with:

- **other people:** we worry about what they think of us
- **ourselves:** we want to find identity and meaning in our lives
- **God:** we want to prove ourselves so that He is pleased with us.

8. When have you seen these pressures to be busy in yourself or other people?

9. What does David think of human reputations?

⊡ apply

10. "My salvation and my honour depend on God" (v 7). How does this truth set us free from worrying about our reputation with:

• other people?

• ourselves?

• God?

⊡ getting personal

When we're daunted by a big or difficult task, we often take refuge in other things. We may reach for the biscuit tin to give some quick pleasure; or do little tasks or play solitaire to give a quick sense of achievement; or create fantasies where we're powerful and successful. What do you do to take refuge? What are you taking refuge from? Where should you look for refuge? **See verses 5-7.**

⊡ investigate

Read v 10-12. We're often too busy because we want wealth or success.

11. When have you seen these pressures to be busy in yourself or other people?

12. What warning does David give to people who live for wealth and success?

⊟ apply

David ends by declaring two great truths about God: God is loving and God is strong (v 11-12). A lot of our over-busyness is caused by our failure really to believe, and then to live out, one of these two truths.

13. What happens when we forget that God is loving?

14. What happens when we forget that God is strong?

⊡ getting personal

This psalm has a refrain that is repeated in verses 1-2 and verses 5-6. In verse 1 David says: "My soul finds rest in God alone". But in verse 5 he commands himself: "Find rest, O my soul, in God alone". Do you need to command your soul? What do you need to tell yourself? What truths about God do you need to preach to yourself?

⬆ pray

Find all the things that Psalm 62 says about God. Praise God for these truths. Confess the times you do not believe and live them out in practice.

5 Psalm 34
A SONG FOR FEARFUL THURSDAYS

⊕ talkabout

1. When are you worried about what other people think of you? When are you afraid of other people's disapproval?

2. What symptoms does this fear of other people produce in you?

⊙ investigate

❯ Read 1 Samuel 21 v 10-15

3. The story describes the situation in which Psalm 34 was written. What fears does David have?

DICTIONARY

Saul (v 10): at this stage he was the king of Israel, and was trying to kill David.

1 Samuel 21 v 12 says David was "very much afraid". Psalm 34 seems to be David's reflection on this fear of the Philistine king. He meditates on how believers should respond to their fears.

> **Read Psalm 34 v 1-10**

4. What does David say about fear in v 1-10?

DICTIONARY

Abimelech (author's note): confusingly, another name for Achish, the king in 1 Samuel 21!
Extol (v 1): praise with enthusiasm.
Saints (v 9): God's people.

5. What does David say about God in v 1-10?

➡ apply

6. We often fear other people because we are looking to them for approval, or because we are worried they will make us feel ashamed. Look at v 5. Where does David say we should look? What happens when we do?

7. We often fear other people because of what they might do to us or withhold from us. We look to other people to provide approval, love, protection or blessing. Look at verses 7-10. Where does David say we should look for these things? What happens when we do?

8. David says the LORD is good, and that He provides every good thing we need (v 8, 10). How is God's provision better than that of other people?

getting personal

Think about the people you fear or whose approval you crave. Think about what they provide for you. It might be approval, love, protection or blessing. How does God provide these things for you? Imagine this person standing next to God. Who is to be feared the most? Who can provide for you the best? "Taste and see that the LORD is good; blessed is the man who takes refuge in him" (v 8).

⊡ **investigate**

> **Read Psalm 34 v 11-22**

9. Look at verse 11. David says we can learn to fear the LORD. What does this actually mean in practice?

DICTIONARY

Fear (v 11): be in awe of.

10. How will we behave if we fear other people more than we fear God?

11. Look at verses 12-14.
How will we behave if we fear God more than we fear other people?

12. Look at verses 15-22. What will God do for those who fear Him?

13. What will God do for those who do not fear Him?

→ apply

14. The LORD delivers His people, says David, "from all their troubles" (v 17). Yet bad things do happen to Christians—often at work. How can we reconcile this promise with the reality of life in the workplace?

15. How have you seen God protecting you at work? How have you seen God using bad experiences at work to make you more like Jesus?

⬆ pray

Think of the people whose rejection you fear or whose approval you crave. Praise God that He is bigger and better than those people. Pray that you might learn to fear God, rather than fearing other people.

6 Psalm 65
A SONG FOR FANTASTIC FRIDAYS

⊕ talkabout

1. When was the last time you had a fantastic day at work? What happened?

⊕ investigate

> **Read Psalm 65**

2. What is the problem that David describes in v 1-4?

3. What is the remedy?

4. Look at verse 4. What is the result?

Because of Good Friday, every Friday (and every other day of the week) is fantastic. We may not always have a great day at work, but we can always rejoice that our sins are forgiven and we can come near to God.

optional

⊡ explore more

> **▶ Read Luke 10 v 17-22**

The disciples return from their work with joy (v 17).

What gives the disciples joy?
What gives Jesus joy?
What does Jesus say should make the disciples rejoice?
Why should we Christians rejoice when we return from work?

5. Look at verses 5-8. What links does David make between God's power in creation and God's power to protect His people?

6. Where, when and for who is God's power available?

⊡ apply

7. What "awesome deeds of righteousness" can God do (or has He already done) in your workplace?

⊡ **investigate**

8.   Look at verses 9-13. What are the signs of abundance in these verses?

Ancient Israel was a farming society. A good year of work = a good harvest. This song may have been written to celebrate a good year—a year crowned with bounty (v 11).

9.   How does the writer explain where this abundance comes from?

⊡ **apply**

10.   When you have a good day or a good year, how do you explain the reason for your success to yourself, and to others?

11. So how should you respond to a good day at work?

⊡ getting personal

Verse 1 says: "Praise awaits you, O God, in Zion". Is praise waiting for God in your heart? Is praise waiting for God when your group meets? Do you talk to one another about God's abundant forgiveness and provision? Or do you moan about your day at work?

Psalm 65 looks back on a good year. But it also looks forward. Verse 8 says all humanity (including those living far away) will sing for joy. Verse 13 says that all creation will sing for joy. It looks forward to a renewed humanity living in a renewed creation. This is possible because God has atoned for our transgressions (v 3-4). Every brilliant and wonderful thing in this life is a pointer to the abundance of life in the new creation.

12. So how can this psalm help us when we have a bad day at work?

⊡ explore more

optional

> **Read Isaiah 65 v 17-25**

How does Isaiah describe work in the new heavens and the new earth?

⊡ explore more

The day after a fantastic Friday or a frightful Friday is Saturday—the Jewish Sabbath day of rest. The Sabbath was a reminder that there was more to life than work. We work and we rest for the glory of God.

> **▶ Read Hebrews 4 v 1-11**

To what does the Sabbath day point?
How can we enter God's Sabbath rest?

⬆ pray

Use this hymn by Adelaide Anne Procter (1825-1864) as the basis of your prayers:

- Use verses 1-2 to thank God for good days at work.
- Use verses 3-4 to pray that we might respond to bad days in the right way.
- Use verses 5-6 to thank God for the rest that awaits us in the new creation.

1. My God, I thank thee, who hast made the earth so bright,
So full of splendour and of joy, beauty and light;
So many glorious things are here, noble and right.

2. I thank thee, too, that thou hast made joy to abound;
So many gentle thoughts and deeds circling us round,
That in the darkest spot of earth some love is found.

3. I thank thee more that all our joy is touched with pain;
That shadows fall on brightest hours; that thorns remain;
So that earth's bliss may be our guide, and not our chain.

4. For thou, who knowest, Lord, how soon our weak heart clings,
Hast given us joys, tender and true, yet all with wings;
So that we see, gleaming on high, diviner things.

5. I thank thee, Lord, that thou hast kept the best in store;
We have enough, yet not too much to long for more:
A yearning for a deeper peace not known before.

6. I thank thee, Lord, that here our souls, though amply blest,
Can never find, although they seek, a perfect rest;
Nor ever shall, until they lean on Jesus' breast.

work songs

Exploring frustration, compromise, stress and joy from the Psalms

LEADER'S GUIDE

Work Songs: Leader's Guide

INTRODUCTION

Leading a Bible study can be a bit like herding cats—everyone has a different idea of what the passage could be about, and a different line of enquiry that they want to pursue. But a good group leader is more than someone who just referees this kind of discussion. You will want to:

- correctly understand and handle the Bible passage. But also...

- encourage and train the people in your group to do this for themselves. Don't fall into the trap of spoon-feeding people by simply passing on the information in the Leader's Guide. Then...

- make sure that no Bible study is finished without everyone knowing how the passage is relevant for them. What changes do you all need to make in the light of the things you have been learning? And finally...

- encourage the group to turn all that has been learned and discussed into prayer.

Your Bible-study group is unique, and you are likely to know better than anyone the capabilities, backgrounds and circumstances of the people you are leading. That's why we've designed these guides with a number of optional features. If they're a quiet bunch, you might want to spend longer on talkabout. If your time is limited, you can choose to skip explore more, or get people to look at these questions at home. Can't get enough of Bible study? Well, some studies have optional extra homework projects. As leader, you can adapt and select the material to the needs of your particular group.

So what's in the Leader's Guide? The main thing that this Leader's Guide will help you to do is to understand the major teaching points in the passage you are studying, and how to apply them. As well as guidance on the questions, the Leader's Guide for each session contains the following important sections:

THE BIG IDEA

One key sentence will give you the main point of the session. This is what you should be aiming to have fixed in people's minds as they leave the Bible study. And it's the point you need to head back towards when the discussion goes off at a tangent.

SUMMARY

An overview of the passage, including plenty of useful historical background information.

OPTIONAL EXTRA

Usually this is an introductory activity that ties in with the main theme of the Bible study, and is designed to "break the ice" at the beginning of a session. Or it may be a "homework project" that people can tackle during the week.

So let's take a look at the various different features of a Good Book Guide:

⊕ talkabout

Each session kicks off with a discussion question, based on the group's opinions or experiences. It's designed to get people talking and thinking in a general way about the main subject of the Bible study.

⊡ investigate

The first thing you and your group need to know is what the Bible passage is about, which is the purpose of these questions. But watch out—people may come up with answers based on their experiences or teaching they have heard in the past, without referring to the passage at all. It's amazing how often we can get through a Bible study without actually looking at the Bible! If you're stuck for an answer, the Leader's Guide contains guidance on questions. These are the answers to direct your group to. This information isn't meant to be read out to people—ideally, you want them to discover these answers from the Bible for themselves. Sometimes there are optional follow-up questions (see ⊗ in guidance on questions) to help you help your group get to the answer.

⊡ explore more

These questions generally point people to other relevant parts of the Bible. They are useful for helping your group to see how the passage fits into the "big picture" of the whole Bible. These sections are OPTIONAL—only use them if you have time. Remember that it's better to finish in good time having really grasped one big thing from the passage, than to try and cram everything in.

⊡ apply

We want to encourage you to spend more time working at application—too often, it is simply tacked on at the end. In the Good Book Guides, apply sections are mixed in with the investigate sections of the study. We hope that people will realise that application is not just an optional extra, but rather, the whole purpose of studying the

Bible. We do Bible study so that our lives can be changed by what we hear from God's word. If you skip the application, the Bible study hasn't achieved its purpose.

These questions draw out practical lessons that we can all learn from the Bible passage. You can review what has been learned so far, and think about practical differences that this should make in our churches and our lives. The group gets the opportunity to talk about what they personally have learned.

⊡ getting personal

These can be done at home, but it is well worth allowing a few moments of quiet reflection during the study for each person to think and pray about specific changes they need to make in their own lives. Why not have a time for reporting back at the beginning of the following session, so that everyone can be encouraged and challenged by one another to make application a priority?

⊡ pray

In Acts 4 v 25-30 the first Christians quoted Psalm 2 as they prayed in response to the persecution of the apostles by the Jewish religious leaders. Today however, it's not as common for Christians to base prayers on the truths of God's word as it once was. As a result, our prayers tend to be weak, superficial and self-centred rather than bold, visionary and God-centred.

The prayer section is based on what has been learned from the Bible passage. How different our prayer times would be if we were genuinely responding to what God has said to us through His word.

1 Psalm 8

A SONG FOR YOUR JOURNEY TO WORK

THE BIG IDEA
Our work is significant because through our work we can glorify God.

SUMMARY
Compared with God and the universe He has made, humanity seems small and insignificant (v 1-4). But God has given us a position of honour. He made us to rule over His world, under Him (v 5-9). Work is one of the key ways we fulfil this role.

Hebrews 2 quotes from this psalm. It recognises that humanity's rule over God's world is corrupted and limited. We do not rule as we should because we do not rule under God.

Jesus entered our humanity to restore our position of honour. He will rule over the world as God intended. In the meantime Christians find a renewed commitment to working for God's glory. We serve God through our work and commend the gospel to others.

GUIDANCE ON QUESTIONS
1. How do you usually feel on your journey to work in the morning? You could also invite people to do some word association with the word "work".

2. Why do you work? Explore what motivates people to work in addition to the need to earn a living.

3. Look at v 1-3. God is a worker (v 3). How do we see the majesty of God's name in what He has made? Get people to share experiences of how creation has moved them to reflect on God's greatness.

4. How should we respond to God's work (v 2)? God is to be praised from the highest heavens (v 1) and the lowest of people (v 2).

5. APPLY: God is a worker! How can that truth change our attitude to work? Work has often been viewed as demeaning or undignified. People with wealth or power have avoided work. But God does not avoid work. This shows that work can be a worthy and noble activity.

EXPLORE MORE
(In Matthew 21 v 1-17) How does Jesus use Psalm 8 v 2 to rebuke the religious leaders?
Why does He do so?
What does the rest of Psalm 8 v 2 add to our understanding of what is happening in Matthew 21?
The blind and lame were normally excluded from the temple (see 2 Samuel 5 v 8). But Jesus welcomes them and heals them. Children were marginal in the culture of the day. They had no voice. Now they are shouting in the temple. Jesus is overturning the elitist structure of the religious leaders. Moreover the praise of the children is directed towards Jesus. And so the religious leaders object. Jesus uses Psalm 8 to show that it was always God's plan for children to praise Him. He also claims to be the God who is praised in Psalm 8. In Psalm 8 the praise of children silences the enemies

of God. In Matthew 21 the praises of the children, rather than the accusations of the religious leaders, represent the true voice of God's people.

6. Look at v 3-4. What is the point of the comparison between God and humanity that the writer makes? Compared with the vast universe God has made, we are small and insignificant. And compared with God, we are very small and insignificant!

7. Look at v 5-9. What is the position God has given to us in His world? In terms of power we are small in the universe. We are lower than the angels. But God has given us a position of great significance. He has placed us as rulers over His world—everything in it is under our authority.

EXPLORE MORE
(In Psalm 104 v 1-24) What are the signs that God has created an ordered world? What is humanity's place in that order? What is our role?
Psalm 104 emphasises the order of God's world. It cannot be moved from its foundations (v 5). He sets boundaries for earth and water (v 9). In this way He ensures that all of creation is cared for. Look at verse 23. Humanity has a place in this ordered world. Our role is to work each day. This is part of the creation order.

8. APPLY: What significance does this [being given the role of ruling the world under God's rule] give to our work?
Our work is a fulfilment of this position of honour and significance. Human work is part of the outworking of our stewardship of God's creation. We co-operate with God through our work in the management of His world.

9. APPLY: How would you rate humanity's performance as stewards of God's world?
- There are many positives. Humanity has created much of great beauty and produced much by way of technological and scientific advancement.
- But environmental damage, poverty and the misuse of technology show that humanity has also abused its role. We do not rule under God as God rules.
- We not only believe Satan's lie that God's rule is oppressive (Genesis 3 v 1-7), we also let it shape the way we rule the world.

10. (Read Hebrews 2 v 5-9.) Look at v 8. What is the writer's verdict on humanity's stewardship? V 6-8 quotes from Psalm 8. "Him" is "man" in the sense of humanity as a whole. Verse 8 contrasts God's intention at creation ("nothing that is not subject to him") with the reality now ("we do not see everything subject to him"). Humanity's rule is both corrupt and limited.

11. What is God's solution (v 9)? See also 1 Corinthians 15 v 20-28. Jesus entered our humanity by becoming a man. He is a new Adam (see 1 Corinthians 15 v 21-22). The first Adam did not rule over creation as God intended. The second Adam will rule over creation as God intended. He will restore humanity's honoured position.

⌄

- **Compare what Psalm 8 says about humanity with what Hebrews 2 v 9 says about Jesus.** Jesus is the perfect human, who rules perfectly, as humanity was meant to.

12. APPLY: How will our hope in Jesus transform the way we think about our work? See Romans 8 v 19-22. Through Jesus, humanity will one day once again rule over the world as God intended. Our rule under God will bring blessing and liberation to the rest of creation.

13. APPLY: How should following Jesus transform our work in the present? See also Colossians 3 v 22-25 and Titus 2 v 9-10. Christians discover a renewed commitment to working for the glory of God. We work as if God is our boss because He is. We work as those who are fulfilling the position God gave as stewards of His world. We work to serve other people and glorify God. In this way Christians can "make the teaching about God our Saviour attractive" (Titus 2 v 10).

OPTIONAL EXTRA

Collect together some quotes on the theme of work including those praising work, cynical about the value of work and humorous. Invite people to comment on the quotes. Search for "work" at www.quotationspage.com or www.askoxford.com/dictionaries/quotation_dict

During each session, ask a member of the group to talk about their work—the temptations it brings and the opportunities it provides—so that you can pray for them in specific ways.

2 Psalm 5

A SONG FOR MISERABLE MONDAYS

THE BIG IDEA
God is with us in the workplace.

SUMMARY
Often Christians can feel as if there is a gap between church on Sundays and work on Mondays. We may even behave in different ways in these different contexts. Psalm 5 recognises that life in an ungodly context is hard. But it reminds us that God is with us in the workplace and that He hears our prayers.

Many people overwork because they are trying to find fulfilment, identity, meaning or approval through their work. Others resort to intrigues and deceit to get ahead or put other people down to look good. But we do not need to prove or justify ourselves because God approves of us and justifies us (makes us right) through the work of Jesus.

GUIDANCE ON QUESTIONS
1. What problems do you face as a Christian in the workplace? Encourage your group to talk about problems that arise because of their faith (rather than general problems they would face anyway even if they weren't believers).

2. How do v 1-3 help us bridge the gap between Sunday and Monday mornings? V 2: God is "my King and my God". God is sovereign over your workplace as well as your church. V 3: God hears us every morning. God hears us on Monday morning as well as Sunday morning. Prayer and the presence of God are as real in the workplace as they are in a church building.

3. Imagine verses 4-6 were displayed on the wall of your workplace. What difference would they make? What difference would they make to you? Ask members to give specific ways these words would help.

4. Look at v 7 and John 2 v 19-22. What does it mean for us today to bow towards the temple? The temple was the symbol of God's presence among His people and a reminder that sinful people can only approach God by having their sins dealt with through sacrifice. See 1 Kings 8 v 27-30. God promised to help His people when they prayed towards the temple. Jesus is the fulfilment of the temple. He is God with us. And He is the sacrifice which covers our sin. We can approach God in the name of Jesus (Hebrews 4 v 14-16). God helps us when we pray to Him in the name of Jesus. This is how we "bow towards the temple" today.

5. Look at v 7-8. What is the solution to living among wicked people? We are to remember God's presence with us and Christ's sacrifice for us (see the comments on Q4). We are to ask God to lead us and keep us on the right path.

6. Look at v 6 and 9-10. What lies are told at your workplace? Encourage people to think not only of explicitly deceitful statements, but false values. For example, people may assume success = climbing the corporate ladder or clinching the deal at any cost. People may assume that, because everyone does it, it is okay to bend the rules.

7. APPLY: Look at verses 11-12. How can we be distinctive in a world often filled with deceit, intrigues and gossip? We are to trust God and rejoice in Him. God will bless us and favour us.

⌄

- **What does this mean in practice?** We practise deceit, intrigues and gossip because we think they bring success (success in our roles or acceptance by colleagues). We put our trust in these things. We need, instead, to put our trust in God. We may also need to redefine success. True success is the blessing God gives = to know Him and His favour.

8. APPLY: Look at verse 3. How often do we need to renew a God-centred perspective on our workplace? How can we do this? Morning by morning we need to renew a God-centred perspective on our workplace and ask Him for help. Share ideas for how we can do this. Are there ways, for example, that people could use the journey to work to refocus on God?

9. Romans 3 v 9-20 quotes Psalm 5 and other Bible references—to show what? No one is righteous. Paul is arguing that Jews as well as Gentiles are not righteous. "Are we (Jews) any better (than the Gentiles)?" (v 9). And the answer is: "No, no one is righteous".

10. How can we be righteous, according to this passage? Only through the righteousness or faithfulness of Jesus. Jesus died as a sacrifice of atonement. He took our unrighteousness and the punishment we deserve on Himself. As a result, we are redeemed from our unrighteousness. We are counted right with God through faith. Or to

put it the other way round—God is pleased with us if we trust in Jesus.

11-12. APPLY: How do you see this in your colleagues? How do you see this in yourself? Most of us find it easier to spot this in others than ourselves! Make sure you spend longer on Q12 than Q11.

13. APPLY: What difference can the good news of justification by faith make in your workplace? Many of us overwork because we are trying to find fulfilment, identity, meaning or approval through our work. Others of us resort to intrigues and deceit to get ahead. Or we may try to look good by putting other people down through gossip. But we can never justify ourselves. It is a futile and endless task. Christians can also feel the need to prove themselves. But understanding justification by faith will transform these attitudes. The problem is that we may believe in justification at the end of time, but not for this week in our workplace. See Matthew 11 v 28-30.

OPTIONAL EXTRA

Beforehand, ask everyone where they will be or what they will be doing at 10 am on the next work-day morning. Then see if people can match up the descriptions with the members of the group. You may have to word the descriptions cleverly to ensure it is not too easy.

3 Psalm 37
A SONG FOR TEMPTING TUESDAYS

THE BIG IDEA

Instead of finding "success" at work through compromise, we should find delight in God.

SUMMARY

We are often tempted to compromise our Christian values in the workplace: to scheme a little (v 7, 12); to take advantage of others (v 14); to be economical with the truth. We see other people who do these things getting on as a result. Even if we don't compromise, we may get angry that others get away with it or worry about the consequences to us (v 8).

In Psalm 37 David tells us not to fret about or envy the success of the wicked (v 1). Often they do succeed in the short-term (v 1, 7, 35), but in the long-term God will judge them (v 2, 9, 10, 13, 15, 17, 20, 22, 32-33, 34, 36, 38). Instead, we should trust and delight in the LORD (v 1-7). We can trust God instead of bending the rules like other people. We should delight in the LORD instead of having the same ambitions as other people.

The land is a prominent feature of this psalm. The righteous will inherit the land, and find peace and blessing in the land. Jesus quotes from this psalm in Matthew 5 v 5, but changes it to speak of the earth. The promise of the land becomes the promise of a new earth. Christians will not always "succeed" in the workplace by worldly definitions of success, but we will inherit a place in God's new creation when Christ returns.

GUIDANCE ON QUESTIONS

1. What temptations do you face at work? Be alert for any pastoral concerns that this question may throw up with your group. People may talk about temptations they face in a veiled way, when they are already succumbing to them. If anyone is particularly struggling with sexual or honesty issues, try to meet with them privately to support them.

2. What do the wicked do (try to find at least six things)? See verses 1, 7, 12, 14, 21, 32.

3. What happens to the wicked in the short term? See verses 1, 7 and 35.

4. How have you seen people getting on in life by doing wrong? This is an opportunity for people to make links between the psalm and their own experience. Encourage people to tell their stories.

5. What happens to the wicked in the long term? See verses 2, 9, 10, 13, 15, 17, 20, 22, 32-33, 34, 36, 38. If you have time, you may want to work through all these references so that their cumulative force strikes people.

6. When will this happen? Sometimes the wicked have a disastrous fall in their own lifetime.

- **When have you seen this happen in your own experience?** You could highlight cases that have made the news. When have you seen verses 14-15 happen—ie: someone caught out by their own scheming?

Often, however, the wicked do not fall within their lifetimes. They die rich and successful. But God will judge all humanity at the end of time (see Hebrews 9 v 27).

7. What does David say the Lᴏʀᴅ will do for the righteous? See verses 4, 6, 9, 11, 18-19, 22, 23-26, 27-28, 34, 37, 39-40. You may want to focus on just some of these references.

8. Look at verses 1-7. How are we to relate to the Lord? We are to trust the Lᴏʀᴅ (v 3); to delight in the Lᴏʀᴅ (v 4); to commit ourselves to the Lᴏʀᴅ (v 5) and to wait on the Lᴏʀᴅ (v 7).

9. APPLY: What does this mean for you in your work situation? Encourage people to see trusting and delighting in the Lᴏʀᴅ as alternatives to compromise with wickedness. We should trust God instead of bending the rules like other people. We should delight in the Lᴏʀᴅ instead of having the same ambitions as other people.

10. APPLY: Look at v 8-9. How do you feel when you see other people getting on in life by doing wrong? We often get angry that others get away with it or we fret about the consequences to us.

11. APPLY: How can trusting and delighting in God help you cope better with these feelings? We get angry because we want to get on or be secure, but we see these desires thwarted by the wickedness of others. Trusting and

delighting in God means our desire to know and serve God becomes stronger than our desires to get on at work.

12. What is the desire of the person described in verse 4? What is God's promise to them? At first sight verse 4 can look like a promise that God will give whatever we want in an indulgent way. But this promise is made to someone whose delight is God Himself. God promises to gives Himself to those who delight in Him. Knowing God is better than anything we might gain by compromising at work.

13. Look for references in the psalm to the promised land. In verses 3, 9, 11, 22, 29 and 34 God promises the land to the righteous. In verses 11 and 37 he promises peace or rest in the land. Verse 18 talks about the inheritance of the blameless, which is a reference to their portion of the land. Verses 18-19, 25-26 and 27 speak of blessing in the land. And in verses 10, 20, 28-29, 36, 38 the wicked vanish or are cut off—a reference to exile from the land.

14. Jesus quotes from this psalm in Matthew 5 v 5. What does He do to the promise of blessing in the land? Jesus makes the promise of the land bigger! He promises the whole earth to His people.

15. What is the future for those who trust in the Lᴏʀᴅ? This psalm does not promise success at work to those who trust in the Lᴏʀᴅ. Indeed it reminds us that often in this present life the wicked get on at the expense of the righteous. But it does promise that those who trust in the Lᴏʀᴅ will share in the new heavens and the new earth when Christ returns in glory.

16. What are you going to remember from this psalm? Encourage each group member to think of something specific (perhaps encourage them to write it down before sharing it with the other members).

17. How are you going to remember it in your workplace next time you are tempted to compromise? Possibilities: write the verse down and keep it on the desk/screen; set an alarm to remind you at times you know you struggle in your day; memorise a verse; associate it with a particular item in your workspace/office.

4 Psalm 62

A SONG FOR WORKAHOLIC WEDNESDAYS

THE BIG IDEA

Much of our over-busyness is caused by our failure to believe the truth about God.

SUMMARY

"My soul finds rest in God alone," says David at the start of Psalm 62. But our work lives are often characterised by busyness and stress. We live in a workaholic culture.

It is not bad to be busy. We are to work for the glory of God, serving Him and other people wholeheartedly. The Bible commends hard work. But the Bible also commends rest. We are to balance work and rest within each week.

David addresses three of the most common reasons why we are too busy:

• We worry about the future or we want to be in control—v 1-4.

• We worry about our reputation—v 5-9.

• We want wealth and success—v 10-12.

The answer is to trust God's control over the future, look to God to honour us and find our delight in God.

David ends by saying two big things about God: God is loving and God is strong (v 11-12). Much of our over-busyness arises because we forget one of these two truths. If we forget God is loving, we may try to prove ourselves (rather than trusting God's grace), or we may look for fulfilment in wealth or success (rather than delighting in God's goodness). If we forget God is strong, we may worry about the future, or try to control our lives (rather than trusting God's sovereignty).

GUIDANCE ON QUESTIONS

1. Why is life today so busy? People may list external factors behind people's busyness: the demands of work, the time spent commuting, and so on. Encourage people to explore the internal pressures or desires that make us busy.

⊻

• **What are the desires in our hearts that make us too busy?** For example: the desire for control, wealth, approval or self-justification.

2. Is it bad to be busy? No. We are to work for the glory of God, serving Him and other people wholeheartedly. See 2 Thessalonians 3 v 6-13. The Bible commends hard work. But the Bible also commends rest. See Exodus 20 v 8-11. We are to balance work and rest within each week. Our work lives are often characterised by over-busyness and stress. We live in a workaholic culture.

3. Where have you seen these pressures to be busy in yourself or other people? This is an opportunity for your group to talk about these issues in a more personal, "closer to home" way.

4. What particular problems did David face? See v 3-4. David faced people who wanted to depose him. People were plotting against him.

5. How would you expect someone to react in this situation? People can run away, hide, or find comfort in the bottle, eating or friends.

6. But how does David react in this situation? See verses 1-2.

7. Why does David react in this way? David can rest in the face of threat because he trusts in God's protection.

⊗

• **Look at the way David repeats the word "my". How does speaking these truths out loud give him confidence?**

EXPLORE MORE
(From Psalm 127 v 1-2) Do you often get up early to get ahead? Or often stay up late to finish?
What's Solomon's verdict on worry-induced overwork? What's his remedy? Everyone has unexpected crises from time to time which mean they have to work long hours. But if this often happens, it is usually a sign that something is wrong. Solomon says getting up early or staying up late can be a sin if it is caused by worry. It results from a failure to trust God. People who trust God sleep well (v 2)!
(From v 3-5) Do you worry about your family's future? What behaviour does this worry produce? What do you think Solomon would say to you? Families are often a source of worry. This worry may make us over-bearing (trying to control people) or over-busy (trying to control circumstances). Instead we should trust God.

8. When have you seen these pressures [ie: worrying about our reputation] to be busy in yourself or other people?

9. What does David think of human reputations? See verse 9.

10. APPLY: "My salvation and my honour depend on God" (v 7). How does this truth set us free from worrying about our reputation with:
• **other people?** We do not have to worry about what other people think of us. We should fear God more than people and God accepts us in Christ.

• **ourselves?** We do not need to find meaning and identity through our activity and achievement. God gives us a new identity in Christ. We are children of God.

• **God?** We do not need to prove ourselves to God. He loved us while we were still His enemies and He makes us right in His sight through Christ.

11. When have you seen these pressures [ie: desiring wealth or success] to be busy in yourself or other people?

12. What warning does David give to people who live for wealth and success? David warns us not to set our hearts on wealth. See Matthew 6 v 19-24. Instead, our delight should be in God.

13. APPLY: What happens when we forget that God is loving? We may try to prove ourselves rather than trusting God's grace. Or we may look for fulfilment in wealth or success rather than delighting in God's goodness.

14. APPLY: What happens when we forget that God is strong? We may worry about the future or try to control our lives rather than trusting God's sovereignty.

OPTIONAL EXTRA

Use this "over-busyness test" together.

1. Do you regularly work thirty minutes a day longer than your contracted hours?
2. Do you check work emails and phone messages at home?
3. Has anyone ever said to you: "I didn't want to trouble you because I know how busy you are"?
4. Do your family or friends complain about not getting time with you?
5. If tomorrow evening was unexpectedly freed up, would you use it to work or do a household chore?
6 Do you often feel tired during the day or find your neck and shoulders aching?
7. Do you often exceed the speed limit while driving?
8. Do you make use of any flexible working arrangements offered by your employers?
9. Do you pray with your children regularly?
10. Do you have enough time to pray?
11. Do you have a hobby in which you are actively involved?
12. Do you eat together as a family or household at least once a day?

If you mainly answered "yes" to questions 1–7 and "no" to questions 8–12, then maybe you have a busyness problem.

See also:
The Busy Christian's Guide to Busyness
by Tim Chester.
Available from
www.thegoodbook.co.uk
tel: 0345 225 0880

5 Psalm 34

A SONG FOR FEARFUL THURSDAYS

THE BIG IDEA

Instead of being controlled by the reactions of work colleagues, we should recognise that God is bigger and better.

SUMMARY

The fear of others is a big factor in most people's lives. We fear rejection or crave approval. Symptoms include susceptibility to peer pressure, over-busyness (because we can't say "no"), "needing" affirmation, telling white lies to cover up our shortcomings, and other people's responses to us making us angry, depressed or anxious.

• God's forgiveness takes away shame and the fear of exposure (v 1-10).

• God's protection takes away the fear of harm (v 11-22).

We must learn to fear God rather than people (v 11).

The background to Psalm 34 is 1 Samuel 21. David was anointed the next king of Israel while King Saul was still on the throne. Saul tries to kill David and so David flees to the Philistine king. The servants of the Philistine king point out that this is the man who killed many Philistine soldiers in battle. So David, fearing for his life, pretends to be mad and the king lets him go. The Philistine king in 1 Samuel 21 is called "Achish" whereas Psalm 34 calls him "Abimelech". "Abimelech" means "my father is king" and so it is possible that "Abimelech" was a general name of the Philistine king (just as "Pharaoh" was a general name for the Egyptian king).

GUIDANCE ON QUESTIONS

1. When are you worried about what other people think of you? When are you afraid of other people's disapproval? Give your group plenty of time to think this one through.

2. What symptoms does this fear of other people produce in you? Think about both how people feel internally, and how they act externally.

3. The story (1 Samuel 21 v 10-15) describes the situation in which Psalm 34 was written. What fears does David have? He fears the harm that the Philistine king can do to him. He probably fears for his life. And so he chooses a course of action (pretending to be insane) that means other people will despise him. He chooses shame.

4. What does David say about fear in Psalm 34 v 1-10? See v 4, 7, 9. God delivers us from our fears. We should fear God. When we fear God, He will protect us and provide for us.

5. What does David say about God in v 1-10? God is worthy of our praise (v 1-3). God answers us when we seek Him. He delivers us from our fears and protects us from danger (v 4-7). God is good and provides good things for those who take refuge in Him (v 8-10).

6. APPLY: We often fear other people because we are looking to them for approval, or because we are worried they will make us feel ashamed. Look

at v 5. Where does David say we should look? What happens when we do? Imagine David pretending to be insane. It must have been humiliating. But David is not worried about what other people think of him. He is not looking to other people for their reaction. He is looking to God for God's reaction. Because we are righteous through faith, we have no reason to feel shame.

7. APPLY: We often fear other people because of what they might do to us or withhold from us. We look to other people to provide approval, love, protection or blessing. Look at verses 7-10. Where does David say we should look for these things? What happens when we do? We should look to the LORD. God protects those who fear Him (v 7) and gives them good things (v 8-10). Those who look to Him will not lack any good thing.

8. APPLY: David says the LORD is good, and that He provides every good thing we need (v 8, 10). How is God's provision better than that of other people? You could explore this question by looking at some of the specific issues people have raised in discussion. Or you could look at the four things mentioned in Q7: approval, love, protection and blessing.

⊻

• How is the approval of God better than the approval of other people?

9. Look at verse 11. David says we can learn to fear the LORD. What does this actually mean in practice? Think about what David is doing in this psalm. Look, for example, at verses 1-3. We learn to fear God by meditating on His majesty, power and

glory, and by meditating on His goodness towards us. And so we learn to fear God by extolling Him, praising Him, glorifying Him and exalting His name together (v 1, 3).

10. How will we behave if we fear other people more than we fear God? We will be more interested in pleasing them than in pleasing God. As a result, we will do whatever we need to do to receive their approval, love, protection or blessing—even if it means displeasing God. We become a slave to that person's attitude towards us. You may want to think back to people's answers to Q2.

Encourage people to be specific. If we are worried about what others think of us, for example, we may tell "little white lies" about ourselves or exaggerate (see v 13).

11. Look at verses 12-14. How will we behave if we fear God more than we fear other people? Pleasing Him will be more important to us than pleasing other people. As a result, we will behave in a way that pleases God no matter what other people think of us.

12. Look at verses 15-22. What will God do for those who fear Him? V 15: the LORD watches those who fear Him. V 17: the LORD hears the prayers of the righteous. V 18-20, 22: the LORD saves and protects the righteous.

13. What will God do for those who do not fear Him? V 16: the LORD is against those who do evil because they do not fear Him. V 21: evil people will be condemned.

14. APPLY: The LORD delivers His people, says David, "from all their troubles" (v 17). Yet bad things do happen to Christians—often at work. How can we

reconcile this promise with the reality of life in the workplace? David was a fugitive when he wrote this psalm. He knew bad things happen to God's people. But God protected his life until he became king. David's greatest Son and heir, King Jesus, also suffered during His life and at His death. But God raised Him from the dead as Lord and Saviour. We are "in Christ". We often suffer in this life, but God keeps us. Nothing can take our hope of heaven away from us. See 1 Peter 1 v 3-5. Moreover, God uses everything that happens to us for our good = becoming like His Son (Romans 8 v 28-29).

15. APPLY: How have you seen God protecting you at work? How have you seen God using bad experiences at work to make you more like Jesus? Encourage your group not only to recount past experiences, but also to be more actively looking for God's protection and sovereign work in good and bad days at work in future.

6 Psalm 65

A SONG FOR FANTASTIC FRIDAYS

THE BIG IDEA

We should praise God for good days at work, and we should look forward to the abundance of the promised new creation.

SUMMARY

Psalm 65 can be divided into three sections:

1. The pardon of God (v 1-4)
2. The power of God (v 5-8)
3. The provision of God (v 9-13)

The pardon of God reminds us that, whether we have had a good day or a bad day at work, we can rejoice in God's forgiveness.

The power of God reminds us that God can help us in every situation.

The provision of God reminds us that we should praise God for all the successes we see at work.

This song may have originally celebrated a good harvest in Israel (v 11). But it also emphasises God's care over people from all nations (v 2, 5, 8). It ends with creation itself singing God's praises. And it starts with a reminder that God atones for our sin. As such, it looks forward to the day when the effects of sin will be transformed as God creates a new humanity in a new creation.

GUIDANCE ON QUESTIONS

1. When was the last time you had a fantastic day at work? What happened? Invite people to talk about what made it a fantastic day.

2. What is the problem that David describes in v 1-4? Being overwhelmed by sins (v 3).

3. What is the remedy? God atones (makes amends) for our transgressions (v 3). In David's day atonement was made through animal sacrifice. But animal sacrifices were a pointer to, or picture of, the cross of Christ (see Hebrews 9). God atones for our sin through Jesus. Jesus died in our place, bearing the penalty of our sin, so that we can be forgiven.

4. Look at verse 4. What is the result? As a result of Jesus' death, we can come near to God (see Mark 15 v 38). The temple was a picture of God's presence and protection among His people. It pointed to the new creation, where there will be no temple because God Himself will be with His people (see Revelation 21 v 3, 22) and we will enjoy good things in God's presence.

EXPLORE MORE

(In Luke 10 v 17-22) What gives the disciples joy?
What gives Jesus joy?
What does Jesus say should make the disciples rejoice?
Why should we Christians rejoice when we return from work?

The disciples rejoice because they have cast out demons (v 17). Their success makes them rejoice. Jesus rejoices because the Father reveals the truth to little children (v 21). Salvation is not based on human merit or wisdom, but on God's grace. Jesus says the disciples should rejoice that their names are written in His book of life (v 20). Knowing God matters more than success in this world. We can rejoice when we have a good day at work. But we should rejoice even more that God forgives us.

5. Look at verses 5-8. What links does David make between God's power in creation and God's power to protect His people? The God who is strong enough to make mountains (v 6) is the God who is our Saviour, who acts in righteousness (v 5).

⊻

- **How does God use His power in the first half of verse 6?**
- **How does he use His power in the second half of verse 6?**
  God formed the mountains by His power. Now He arms Himself with power. The image is that of a warrior equipped for battle. God is ready to protect His people.

See also v 7. God stills the roaring of the sea and waves. But He also stills the turmoil of the nations. God is powerful over creation and He is powerful over the nations.

6. Where, when and for who is God's power available? In all places, to the ends of the earth and wherever the morning dawns (v 5, 8). It is available at all times, from the first light of the dawn to the last light of the evening (v 8). It is available to all people who call on him (v 5) including "those living far away". "Those living far away" is probably a reference to the Gentiles = non-Jews (see also "all men" in verse 2), but it would also have been a comfort to later generations of Jews living in exile in Babylon.

7. APPLY: What "awesome deeds of righteousness" can God do (or has He already done) in your workplace? This is an opportunity for people to tell stories of God's power in their lives. Reinforce the idea

that God is with us in the workplace—even when He seems far away.

8. Look at verses 9-13. What are the signs of abundance in these verses? God enriches the land abundantly (v 9). He fills the streams and drenches the furrows (v 9-10). He blesses the crops so that the year is crowned with bounty and the carts overflow with produce (v 10-11). The fields overflow so that they are covered with flocks and grain (v 12-13).

9. How does the writer explain where this abundance comes from? From God.

⊻

- **Look at all the references to "you" ie: God. What does the Psalmist says God has done?**

10. APPLY: When you have a good day or a good year, how do you explain the reason for your success to yourself, and to others? Our culture tends to attribute success to the hard work of staff, the creativity of advertisers, the skill of managers or the luck of the market. All of these may be contributing factors. But Psalm 65 encourages us to recognise that God is the ultimate source of all blessing.

11. APPLY: So how should you respond to a good day at work? By praising God, attributing success to Him and rejoicing at His power in our lives. Explore with people what this might involve in practice. For example, you could encourage one another to share successes at work so that the group can praise God.

12. APPLY: So how can this psalm help us when we have a bad day at work?

Not every Friday is fantastic! But, because Psalm 65 also points forward to a new creation, it can comfort us on bad days. It reminds us that a day is coming when work will no longer be frustrating, oppressive or futile. See Isaiah 35 and 55.

EXPLORE MORE
How does Isaiah 65 v 17-25 describe work in the new heavens and the new earth? See verses 21-22. Other people will no longer take the fruit of our labour—work will no longer be oppressive. See verse 23. We will enjoy the fruit of our labours—work will no longer be frustrating or futile. God's vision of a new world includes the world of work. God will redeem and transform human work.

EXPLORE MORE
(From Hebrews 4 v 1-11) To what does the Sabbath day point? The generation that was led out of Egypt by Moses during the exodus did not enjoy rest in the land because of their disobedience (3 v 12-19 and 4 v 6-9). So the promise of rest still waits to be fulfilled (4 v 9-11).
How can we enter God's Sabbath-rest? Rest in the land of Palestine was only a pointer. The Sabbath day was a picture of the Sabbath-rest of God in a new creation for all eternity (4 v 3-5). We can enter the Sabbath-rest of God through faith in the gospel (4 v 1-2, 11). See Revelation 14 v 13.

Also available in the Good Book Guide series...

OLD TESTAMENT

Soul Songs: Psalms
6 studies. ISBN: 9781904889960

David: God's True King
6 studies. ISBN: 9781904889984

Ruth: Poverty and Plenty
4 studies. ISBN: 9781905564910

Ezekiel: The God of Glory
6 studies. ISBN: 9781904889274

Jonah: The Depths of Grace
6 studies. ISBN: 9781907377433

Zechariah: God's Big Plan
6 studies. ISBN: 9781904889267

NEW TESTAMENT
Mark 1-8: The Coming King
10 studies. ISBN: 9781904889281

Mark 9-16: The Servant King
7 studies. ISBN: 9781904889519

Romans 1-5: God and You
6 studies. ISBN: 9781904889618

1 Thessalonians: Living to Please God 7 studies. ISBN: 9781904889533

2 Timothy: Faithful to the End
7 studies. ISBN: 9781905564569

Hebrews: Consider Jesus
8 studies. ISBN: 9781906334420

1 Peter: Living in the Real World
5 studies. ISBN: 9781904889496

Revelation 2-3: A message from Jesus to the church today
7 studies. ISBN: 9781905564682

TOPICAL
Biblical Womanhood 9 studies.
ISBN: 9781904889076

Biblical Manhood 10 studies.
ISBN: 9781904889977

Experiencing God 6 studies.
ISBN: 9781906334437

Women of Faith from the OT
8 studies. ISBN: 9781904889526

Women of Faith from the NT
8 studies. ISBN: 9781905564460

The Holy Spirit 8 studies.
ISBN: 9781905564217

The Apostles' Creed 10 studies.
ISBN: 9781905564415

Contentment 6 studies.
ISBN: 9781905564668

Visit your friendly neighbourhood website to see the full range, and to download samples
UK & Europe: www.thegoodbook.co.uk • N America: www.thegoodbook.com
Australia: www.thegoodbook.com.au • New Zealand: www.thegoodbook.co.nz

thegoodbook
COMPANY

At The Good Book Company, we are dedicated to helping Christians and local churches grow. We believe that God's growth process always starts with hearing clearly what He has said to us through His timeless word—the Bible.

Ever since we opened our doors in 1991, we have been striving to produce resources that honour God in the way the Bible is used. We have grown to become an international provider of user-friendly resources to the Christian community, with believers of all backgrounds and denominations using our Bible studies, books, evangelistic resources, DVD-based courses and training events.

We want to equip ordinary Christians to live for Christ day by day, and churches to grow in their knowledge of God, their love for one another, and the effectiveness of their outreach.

Call us for a discussion of your needs or visit one of our local websites for more information on the resources and services we provide.

www.thegoodbook.co.uk
N America: www.thegoodbook.com
Australia: www.thegoodbook.com.au
New Zealand: www.thegoodbook.co.nz

UK & Europe: 0333 123 0880
N America: 866 244 2165
Australia: (02) 6100 4211
New Zealand (+64) 3 343 1990

www.christianityexplored.org
Our partner site is a great place for those exploring the Christian faith, with a clear explanation of the gospel, powerful testimonies and answers to difficult questions.

One life. What's it all about?